MY LIFE AS A HONEY BEE

Joyce A. Wagner

ISBN 978-1-953223-67-8 (paperback)
ISBN 978-1-953223-66-1 (digital)

Copyright © 2020 by Joyce A. Wagner

All rights reserved. No part of this publication may be reproduced, distributed, or transmitted in any form or by any means, including photocopying, recording, or other electronic or mechanical methods without the prior written permission of the publisher. For permission requests, solicit the publisher via the address below.

Rushmore Press LLC
1 800 460 9188
www.rushmorepress.com

Printed in the United States of America

CONTENTS

Acknowledgment iv
Chapter 1   Our Origin. 1
Chapter 2   Pollination 3
Chapter 3   Honey 9
Chapter 4   Honey Products. 12
Chapter 5   Life in Our Colony 14
Chapter 6   Foraging 18
Chapter 7   Our Honeycomb 20
Chapter 8   Capped Brood 24
Chapter 9   Our duties. 27
Chapter 10   Communication. 31
Chapter 11   How We Recognize Each Other. 33
Chapter 12   Our Diseases and Predators 37
Chapter 13   Propolis. 46
Chapter 14   Our Anatomy. 47
Chapter 15   Beeswax 52
Chapter 16   Honey 54
Chapter 17   Making a Colony: Swarming 56
Chapter 18   How We Winter 61
Chapter 19   Our Friend, the Beekeeper. 62
Chapter 20   Killer Bees. 64
Chapter 21   Coding. 66
Chapter 22   Our Stinger. 67
Chapter 23   Research. 69
Chapter 24   In Conclusion 73
Bibliography. 74

ACKNOWLEDGMENT

My sincerest thanks to Dr. Nancy Greig, Curator of Entomology and Director of the Cockrell Butterfly Center, and her very professional staff at the Houston Museum of Natural Science for their docent training sessions. They were very helpful in teaching me about honey bees and spurred my interest to learn more.

CHAPTER 1
OUR ORIGIN

We honey bees have been around since the Paleocene period and the Eocene-Oligocene epoch, which is about twenty-three to fifty-six million years ago. We haven't changed very much. An ancestor of mine is preserved in pine sap that is estimated to be thirty to forty million years ago, and we look alike! There are paintings in Spain and other parts of Europe that show hunters collecting and harvesting our wild honey. Some paintings are said to be from around 6000 BC. Archeologists have found honey in Egyptian tombs that was edible. Ancient Egyptians and Middle Eastern people used honey for embalming. Romans used honey to pay their taxes. We were highly respected, as proved by our engraved images on ancient coins, symbols for kings and religious leaders, and of course our popularity in mythology. People use our image in jewelry. They seem to prefer ladybugs or dragonflies (or damselflies) to us. We don't know why that is. You also seem to like butterflies a lot.

There are about twenty thousand known species of bees, seven species of honey bees, and forty-four subspecies. We are a subset of bees in the genus *Apis mellifera* and originated in Eastern Africa. We spread to Northern Europe and Eastern Asia before being carried to America. *Apis florea* is one of our subsets and is found in the southern and southeastern parts of Asia and as far north as Japan and Korea. *Apis cerana*, the Eastern honey bee, is from Southern and Eastern Asia. *Apis cerana* is a bit different. They prefer to withdraw from their enemy rather than attack. When necessary, they will surround the invader and increase its temperature to 116 degrees Fahrenheit, and that increase plus the increase in the carbon dioxide level can dispatch an intruder. It's similar to what we do to our queen. We call it "balling the queen." We use our stingers to do it. *Apis dorsata* (the giant honey bee) also belongs to our subspecies and is from South and Southeast Asia.

CHAPTER 2
POLLINATION

We were not the first to pollinate. Beetles were. We evolved from predatory wasps but eons ago switched to pollen gathering. It took centuries for us to develop physical and behavioral adaptations that make us more efficient at pollinating than other insects and birds such as humming birds. Let me tell you a little secret: we love to watch humming birds extract nectar and pollen. We think they look funny. We dive in. They hover ever so daintily. If we collected pollen the way they do, there would be a lot less honey and beeswax in the world. They definitely are not our competitors. We pollinate 80–90 percent of the world's food crops. We don't pollinate grains. If it were not for pollination, many vegetable and fruit plants would not exist. People and animals depend on plants to sustain them. Think of cows and pigs, turkeys and chickens, and all the fruits and vegetables you eat and drink. We're the only species that produce food for humans. That food is honey, and it is the purest food on earth. We also pollinate flowers and plants that you like to look at and pick. Tch tch. That means less pollen and honey for me and you!

MY LIFE AS A HONEY BEE

How do we pollinate? We have to know what, how, when, and where to pollinate. Flavor and color of honey depend on which flowers we visit. Color is the result of the plant's ability to produce substances that protect us from predators, bacteria, and fungi. Our orange and yellow stripes warn predators to stay away from us. It's also why we are so very pretty.

We especially like the colors yellow and blue. A mixture of them also appeals to us. There are other colors that we like, such as orange, brown, and gray. We are able to see ultraviolet (UV) parts of the spectrum that a human can't see. That's a big help on cloudy days.

When cloudy days turn into rainy days, we may still forage. We'll sometimes fly. Sometimes not. It depends on a lot of things, such as the season, flowers, and of course, our supply of honey. If there is a light drizzle, we might fly. If it's a slashing rain that comes crashing down, we'll stay home. Our little wings get too wet, and it's too hard to find pollen and nectar to carry to our hive. Solar radiation, of course, also plays a part in weather changes, so we are affected by radiation.

Aromas attract us. I have an acute sense of smell. I couldn't be an effective foraging bee without it. I have 170 odor receptors that help me find pollen and nectar from flowers that might be miles away. The receptors help us find our kin and communicate within the hive. Each colony has its own odor.

Bad odors like leather, wool, and body odors are obnoxious to us. Sweet smells attract us to you. So no colognes, perfumes, aftershave lotions, hairsprays, etc., etc., etc. If we soar toward you or land on you, it must be because you're wearing one of our favorite colors or we like your scent. In any case, please don't start screaming and thrashing around like a Tasmanian devil.

We'll figure out you're not a flower. All that commotion will truly upset us, and you know what will happen next, don't you!

We look for well-formed flowers that are open and full of nectar and pollen with no deformities because we have to get inside the flower in order to collect nectar (sugar water) and pollen (powder). We have to do our gathering when the flowers are fertile, so we have to be very quick. Flowers don't last long.

We suck up nectar with our proboscis (like your tongue) and store it in our honey sac (also known as a honey stomach or honey crop). As we move about, pollen sticks to our legs. When we go from flower to flower, pollen is transferred between male and female parts of the flower. Pollination, therefore, is fertilization because in the process of pollination, seed develops, and a seed is the start of life.

Pollen is found in raw, natural honey and is rich in vitamin A (carotene), B1 (thiamine), B2 (riboflavin), B3 (nicotinic acid), B5 (pantothenic acid), vitamin C (ascorbic acid), H (biotin), and R (rutin). It is 10 percent sugar, enzymes, carbohydrates, and minerals. It's also 35 percent protein. So it's better than sugar. You can use it as a health supplement and even sprinkle it on your cereal.

Beekeepers help us pollinate by moving our hives from place to place according to where pollination is needed. They do this when a nearby supply of wildflowers is scarce. Nothing new about that. Early Egyptians did it.

We pack pollen in baskets called corbicula on our legs. If you ever see me (or my sisters) hovering and buzzing around a flower, look very closely, and you'll see my hind legs loaded with pollen.

MY LIFE AS A HONEY BEE

Some bees carry pollen on the undersides of their abdomens which are called scopa. The pollen is spread over the entire abdominal area. Either way, when we collect pollen, we have to stop to groom ourselves.

Why do we go through the trouble of pollinating? We get protein from our collection to feed ourselves. Our muscles need the energy we get from protein to keep us from starving and freezing to death in winter. We dine all winter long from our summer collection.

We are programmed to always have a surplus of honey. When our supply gets low, we just forage and make more honey. Furthermore, our beekeeper makes sure we can always feed ourselves year round. We never go hungry. We are very good pollinators.

MY LIFE AS A HONEY BEE

We forage for pollen in weeds like goldenrod, clover, and dandelion and herbs like mint and thyme and bee balm and bachelor's button. We are partial to sunflowers, saliva, and aster. Some bees are not particular what flowers they visit while others are choosy. Of course, it goes without saying that our pollen and nectar gathering doesn't hurt flowers. A combination of pollen and nectar gives a very tasty honey. It's like adding spice to soup.

You know that honey bees migrated to Europe, Africa, and Asia. But do you know how we got to the United States? Pilgrims brought us in the 1600s. Some of us escaped from our hives and winged our way west like the pioneers of the Great Plains. Many times, feral honey bees got to uninhabited regions before the pioneers. Mormons carried us into Utah in the 1800s, and ships brought us to California in the late 1840s.

CHAPTER 3
HONEY

I'm sure you've heard the word honeymoon. Do you know where the word came from? In days long gone, newlyweds drank mead (a mixture of honey, wine, and spices) because they thought it would assure the birth of a son. At one time, mead was a popular drink among royalty. Another example of a popular drink is Drambuie. It's made with honey, whiskey, and spices.

Honey has all the substances people need. And that includes water. There are about 1.04 ounces of water in slightly less than 4 ounces of honey. Honey is made when nectar and pollen are modified by proteins and enzymes. There are 180 different substances in honey that interact in such a way that our honey can't be exactly duplicated.

Honey has good medicinal properties. One way to tell honey's medicinal strength is by its color. The darker the color, the greater is its medicinal properties. It can be used for minor cuts, abrasions, and burns because of its antibacterial and antimicrobial properties. Honey sucks in moisture and produces hydrogen peroxide which speeds up healing. Some researchers are experimenting with putting honey on bandages. It's also better for burns than the standard treatment which is silver sulfadiazine. People who are anemic or have infections can sometimes improve with the use of honey. It's also used to treat acne and eczema.

While honey is an antibiotic, it does contain spores of bacteria that are inert and harmless to adults but not to infants under a year because bacteria grow in the infant's intestines and cause muscle weakness, poor appetite, and irritability. It can cause botulism. If you look on the label of a jar of honey that is 100 percent pure, you will see that honey should not be given to infants.

You may be wondering what we do with the pollen and nectar once they're in the hive and how honey is manufactured from them.

When the scout (foraging) bee returns from a collection, she distributes some of the pollen and nectar she's collected by regurgitating it to a house bee. It takes less than a minute to do this.

How does she regurgitate? She opens her mandible and pushes her proboscis forward to regurgitate some of the nectar that she has stored in her honey stomach into the mouth of a house bee that has pushed her proboscis toward the mouth of the foraging bee. (You're probably going "Yuck.") The house bee ingests and regurgitates (yuck again) the nectar and deposits the nectar on a honeycomb. In other words, we gather pollen, ingest it, mix it with our spittle, spit it out, deposit it, and repeat. Eventually, the nectar becomes honey.

The transfer of food from bee to bee might remind you of two spacecrafts in outer space coupling to transfer equipment or astronauts.

Depending on the beekeeper's tools and equipment, honey is made into different products for profit. That's why our honey is liquid gold.

CHAPTER 4
HONEY PRODUCTS

For example, one product is extracted honey that is made from wax cappings left after liquid is removed by centrifugal force and then strained. It's pretty sticky business. Sometimes we get so sticky the beekeeper has to remove us.

There is comb honey. The entire honeycomb (wax and honey) is simply removed. You can eat the whole thing. It's yummy (so I've heard).

Whipped honey is creamed honey in semisolid form made when granulated honey is blended with extracted liquid. It's very smooth. Think of peanut butter.

Then there is chunk honey. Chunks of honeycomb are put in a container filled with extracted liquid honey. Slice chunk honey and spread it on toast instead of butter.

Don't refrigerate honey. Ever. It crystallizes. Old honey will also crystallize. Also, whatever you use to store honey, be sure it's sealed very tight. Unsealed honey absorbs moisture, becomes diluted, and will ferment. Water and yeast spores cause honey to ferment. It must be pasteurized—i.e., heated to kill the yeast spores. This is why honey has a long shelf life. Of course, foods made with honey stay fresh and moist for a long time because honey absorbs moisture.

Beekeepers constantly check our hive to determine if our hive is filled with cured and capped honey. That's how they know when our honey is ready to be harvested.

You may be wondering how much honey a beekeeper can expect from a hive. Well, how many pounds of honey we make depends on how many bees are in the hive, the weather, rainfall, location of our hive, and how strong our colony is. In a year's time, it's possible we can make about sixteen gallons of honey, or two hundred pounds a year. If our hive is healthy and we have a good-sized colony, we can produce more.

We have to visit about two million flowers in order to get one pound of honey. Usually we have to visit fifty to one hundred flowers on a collection trip. For all the foraging and collecting we do, each one of us only makes one-twelfth teaspoon of honey in our entire lives.

People see and hear us honey bees, but they don't pay any attention to us. We are very important! I really don't know what you would do without us.

CHAPTER 5
LIFE IN OUR COLONY

What's life like in a colony of honey bees? Let me begin with when I entered the hive. I entered a colony with about sixty thousand other bees. That's the usual number. We share a hive with drones and one queen. We have a hierarchy. Nature has programmed us to cooperate with one another. We couldn't thrive and survive without one another's help. Just like you. There is no fighting among us except for the queen bee who won't tolerate a rival. Virgin queens may or may not fight. It depends on a lot of factors, such as population, age of our queens, etc.

There are two female castes in a hive. If you're born female, you're either a worker bee or a queen bee. There is no other option. We are much more numerous than drones.

We female bees have a multitude of work to do and have several duties that overlap in the same period. The duties depend on our age. Our work is never done. I'm sure you have heard the saying "Busy as a bee."

We have some rather unique and interesting ways to communicate with one another, especially when we forage. Dancing is one of them. We love to dance and are great choreographers. Dancing communicates distance and direction and alerts us to when we need to swarm. Dancing is our language. It has some sort of grammar. We never think about that. Scents and vibrations are other ways we use to communicate.

We have seven kinds of dances. We have a round dance, a waggle dance, a sickle dance, a grooming dance, a tremble (or trembling) dance, a jostling dance, and a break dance which is also called a buzzing run. All the dances regulate our behavior and assignments. Not many insects are capable of that kind of communication. We are very intelligent and useful insects.

We use the round dance to let our colony know food is nearby—i.e., it gives distance. After all, we want to know if foraging is worth the effort and risk of flight; and, if so, how far, where, and what the flavors are. Kind of like going to Baskin-Robbins.

In the round dance, foraging bees run in one direction, reverse their direction, and run in a circle that gets wider and wider and wider. It's a loop. They'll do this several times. When the dance is finished, food is again distributed by regurgitating. Then the foraging bees fly out in all directions. Our odor receptors guide us to the flowers where the scout bees left their scent.

In the jostling dance, which is done after we return from foraging and comes before the waggle, we run and push other bees to alert them the waggle dance is about to begin.

The waggle dance replaces the round dance. First, the foragers run straight ahead, return in a half circle, run again, then turn in the opposite direction. It looks like a figure eight pattern. While doing this, they wag their abdomen sideways. It looks like they're wagging their tails. (None of us has one.) It must look peculiar to an observer. We also buzz our wings to communicate.

The waggle dance differs from the round dance in that it is used for food sources at a distance of 490 feet or more from the hive. The straight run indicates direction of food, and the waggle indicates distance. The greater the distance, the longer is the time we spend waggling. The shorter the distance, the less time we spend waggling. We also squeak as we dance.

How fast we waggle, how many times we do it, and the direction (angle of the waggle run is determined by the angle of the sun) as well as the sound we make is very precise and lets foraging bees know where to find food. The quality and quantity of our food source determine how enthusiastic our scout bees are. If the foraging is successful, the scout bees dance very vigorously. So then we know the flowers have pollen and nectar. If their dance is sluggish (or not at all), we know there is no point in leaving the safety and comfort of our hive.

The sickle dance is a transition between the round dance and the waggle dance. But we don't waggle. Its form is more crescent shaped than the figure eight of the waggle dance or the circular pattern of the round dance. It lets us know food is neither too close nor too far away from the hive.

We also have a tremble, or trembling dance, which is similar to the waggle dance. We use this dance when we can't unload our collection or because there is a shortage of bees to receive the booty. We recruit more bees this way. Also, if the bees ignore us, we know there is enough pollen and nectar, so we can relax a bit. This dance can also spread the scent from a forager's waggle dance.

Then there is the break dance. It's also called a buzzing run because we run in a straight line while flapping our wings. We deliberately collide with another bee. We touch antennae, buzz, and run off to hit another bee. So it's a cascading action. We do this before swarming.

If foraging bees consume ethanol (from corn), the tremble dance is increased while the waggle dance is decreased. I've heard you use ethanol as fuel for your cars and in your alcoholic drinks. Rumor is that some of you get quite tipsy when overdoing the juice. This does not happen to us. It would be hilarious if it did. Can you picture us flying (assuming we're able to get off the ground in the first place) into one another, trying to find our hive's entrance? What would we taste like to our predators that we couldn't avoid because our equilibrium is off? Would our guard bees keep us from entering our hive? Would they make us sleep outside the hive? We would have to sleep it off somewhere. Could we forage the day after our binge? Or would we be too hungover?

Our work makes us dusty and sticky. We take care of this in our grooming dance. In this dance, we grip the comb with our legs and rock our bodies side to side as in an arc. Occasionally, we stop rocking and groom our abdomen, thorax, and head with our legs. Usually we have to pivot our bodies to clean all parts. This is not an easy thing for us to do. However, another bee will help us by touching us with her antenna. In other words, the dance is an invitation or a request for assistance. We have to have our bodies clean. Otherwise, we would not be able to forage or go about our other tasks effectively.

We use the sun as our compass. When the sun is to the east, as it is in the morning, we dance straight up, but in the late afternoon, when the sun is to the west, we dance straight down. As the sun moves across the sky, its angle changes. We have to change direction to stay in line with the sun. Because we depend on the sun for direction, we are not very active on cloudy days.

CHAPTER 6
FORAGING

When we return to the hive from foraging, we process the nectar until it becomes honey. We also bring water that we stored in our honey crop back to the hive. We spread the water in a thin film on top of our sealed brood or on larvae cells or eggs. Since nectar can become high in water and yeast, honey will ferment if not treated. We house bees fan to reduce the percentage of water in the nectar.

When I'm ready to forage, I have to imprint my hive's location. It's easy to tell when this happens because I fly up, down, and around in front of the entrance to the hive. I circle the hive. Each time I circle, the orbit gets longer and wider. That's how I learn landmarks.

Foraging is very challenging. We can forage as many as two miles a day,. That's approximately six thousand acres. My entire colony could fly ninety thousand miles if it had to. That's about equal to three orbits around the earth. Despite the distance we travel, we would only use about an ounce of honey.

Foraging is hard work and fatiguing. And very dangerous. It is fraught with all kinds of hazards. When I return from foraging, I carry around 0.00257 ounces of nectar in my stomach. That's about 85 percent of my body weight. As you can imagine, this makes me a bit sluggish. Because my sisters and I get so tired and sluggish and so weighed down with all the pollen and nectar we carry, we're not always able to touch down. Instead, we buy the farm—i.e., we crash land in front of the hive.

Personally, I do not like foraging. I get cold when the sun goes down. I may die on the way home. A bird can eat me. Bugs and spiders hide in flowers to catch me when I'm going about collecting pollen or nectar. (My sisters and I must be very tasty.) My wings can get torn and tattered. My exoskeleton becomes dark in color. That means my skeleton is on the outside. Yours is on the inside. Otherwise, our anatomies are quite similar.

CHAPTER 7
OUR HONEYCOMB

Our houses are beehives. In the beehive we have hexagonal-shaped honeycombs. Why are honeycombs hexagonal shaped? It's mostly a matter of efficiency.

We have to be efficient because we have to get the most work done by the least amount of effort in the shortest time possible. That is the definition of efficiency (getting the maximum work done in the least amount of time with the least amount of effort). That is why we have to be very particular about the shape of our cells, its position to other cells, and how much honey can be stored in each cell. That's why our cells are hexagons.

MY LIFE AS A HONEY BEE

All cells start off as circles. Circles leave gaps. We don't have time to fill in the gaps. We change the shape by heating wax but not until it becomes liquid. The wax resembles lava and is pliable. By using our body temperature and our antennae, mandibles, and legs, we can manipulate the wall comb and cause the cell walls to flatten. That's how we shape cells into a hexagon.

The hexagonal shape uses the least amount of material. There is no space between the cell walls and the cells nestle into each other resulting in each end being shared by another end. If the walls were circular there would be no nesting. You'll notice that our hexagonal cells form a lattice design. You'll also notice that the cells are horizontally aligned and that the cells are not equal and not even the same size. You'll have to look very intently to see that drone cells are broad, queen bell cells are elongated, and the worker bee cells are the smallest.

Hexagons give us the greatest surface area to maximize space between cells while at the same time minimizing space to store our honey and lay our eggs, and they give us the greatest volume so we can store our honey.

Another concern of ours is how to keep honey from dripping all over and making a mess. We angle the cells up. We have enough work to do without having to clean up messy cells.

How we make the cells hexagonal has always baffled such luminaries as Galileo Galilei (who, like Copernicus realized that the sun was stationary and our planet revolved around it) and Johannes Kepler (a skilled mathematician). Both lived in the 1600s.

If your scientists ever figure out how we make the hexagon shape, they might use it in buildings and structural materials.

As you can see, we really are the epitome of engineering and are highly intelligent. (You will excuse my bragging a bit, won't you?)

While on the subject of honeycombs, I should also mention that there are brood combs. These combs get dark over time. One reason is that they get walked over. You call them travel stains. As with all other things, the black comb has to be removed because of pathogens and pests.

We like brood combs because it attracts wild swarms.

By the way, we're not the only ones that make honeycombs. Wasps also make hexagonal cells but they use paper. Bumble bees do not.

Bumble bees don't make honey. They carry nectar from plants they visit. There is no need for them to store food because in the cold they hibernate. So they feast on nectar, pollen, and homemade honey in warmer weather. The food they do store is used for larvae and egg-producing queens. We think they're odd because when they hibernate they can turn into queen bees. They have the ability to do that. So it's only queen bees that hibernate. And, they can hibernate for as long as nine months! Also bumble bees can live above or below ground but they prefer below ground. Their queen will often find an abandoned burrow to breed.

And I won't forget wasps. Those nasty predators. Wasps do not make honey or pollinate crops. Although there are some species of wasps that do make honey for their larvae. They make nests from paper. Not wax combs like we do. Their nests are usually hexagonal-shaped. Like bumble bees they die in winter except for fertile females who become queens. Wasps are carnivores. They eat grasshoppers, caterpillars, bee, spiders, and us. Wasps make their nests from wood that they chew into a paste-like pulp with their saliva.

CHAPTER 8
CAPPED BROOD

Let me now say something about our capped brood because it's important and it's where we develop from an egg to an adult.

Capped brood is located on frames close to the center of the hive. They are larvae cells that have developed from the egg stage. Larvae are distinguished by their C-shape and are worm-like. This is a very vulnerable stage in our development because this is when invaders attack us and we can get diseases or eaten.

In about three days, our eggs hatch into larvae that look like grubs. The larvae grow very rapidly. Our nurse bees feed the larvae bee bread (pollen and honey) 1,300 times a day. They are gluttons. They go into a feeding frenzy. They need nutrition to grow, and they grow very quickly. When they're about as big as they're ever going to be, they're 1,500 times their original size. Larvae are like reptiles because they shed their outer layer. They do this about five times. After molting, the larvae spin a cocoon around their bodies. It's then time to seal the larvae in a cell with porous capping and tan beeswax. We worker bees do this.

The larvae stage is the stage before we develop into pupae and then into adults. In the larvae stage, nurse bees also feed us royal jelly (bee milk), which is loaded with B vitamins, minerals, vitamin A and protein. Royal jelly is made from digested pollen, honey, or nectar and is mixed with a chemical secreted from the hypopharyngeal gland in the nurse bee's head. After the third day, nurse bees feed only the queen bee larvae royal jelly. It's how worker bee and drone eggs become different from queen bee eggs. In other words, our nurse bees help choose which eggs become queen bee eggs and which become worker bee or drone eggs.

No one can see us in the pupae stage because we're hidden under our wax capping. We're like the fetus in humans. In the pupae stage, we begin to look like bees. Our eyes are the first to be colored. They're first pink, then black. Our skeleton forms. Hair develops on our bodies.

Maturation differs depending on whether we are drones, worker bees, or queen bees. For example, a drone takes twenty-four days before they chew their way out of the capping. A worker bee takes twenty-one days and the queen, who lives the longest, takes sixteen days.

It's easy to tell when we're about to emerge from under the capping because you can see us moving. When we break through, we weigh in at about 0.0028 ounces.

MY LIFE AS A HONEY BEE

When we emerge, we're fully developed, exhausted, and hungry. One of the first things we do after chewing our way out of the six-sided, two-sided cell of beeswax that our older worker bees produced is to gorge ourselves with food older worker bees provided for us. Of course, we're a bit wobbly until our legs get strong. However, in no time at all, we stand and walk. Flying comes later.

CHAPTER 9
OUR DUTIES

For half my life, I'm a house bee. Housekeeping is my first duty. My duties at this time are to keep the hive clean. Every cell has to be super clean.

While I'm a house bee, my undertaking duties begin. I do this from day 3 to day 16. This is when I help remove sick bees and bees that have gone to bye-bye land. My sisters and I carry the bees to a safe distance from the hive.

On the fourth to twelfth day, I'm a nurse bee. I nurse the queen and take care of bees that have just chewed their way out of the capping. Like my sisters, I have to encourage the queen to keep laying eggs. When we're nurse bees, we consume large amounts of pollen, nectar, and water. Water is needed so that our hypopharyngeal glands can produce royal jelly used to feed the larvae. We could not survive without water. (Remind you of anyone you know?)

Honey that we've stored in summer for use in winter crystallizes. It gets dry. We need water to turn it back to liquid so we can eat it. We never outlive our use for water. Although we can satisfy our thirst with any kind of water, we prefer water that's a bit slimy green. The beekeeper helps us by seeing that there is water nearby, especially in hot weather when we need to keep our hive at an even temperature.

While we're doing our nursing duties, virgin queens are developing in their pupae stage (from about the fourteenth to the sixteenth day). In this stage, the queens are very fragile.

Shopping and fanning (we're still house bees) occur between the twelfth and eighteenth day. They work together. By shopping, I mean we take nectar from foraging bees and deposit the nectar into special cells that are marked to receive nectar. We also take pollen and pack it into other cells. This is our food.

In summer, our hive has to be cooled, so we furiously fan our wings to circulate air and evaporate water. The less water, the thicker the honey. When we fan, we keep the temperature between ninety-three and ninety-five degrees. Our developing brood needs that high temperature to develop. We take turns fanning because fanning is very exhausting.

Fanning releases an odor from our scent gland at the end of our abdomen. The odor tells foraging bees they're at the right hive. It also helps us find food. So you see, fanning is another way we communicate.

If you look at us through a magnifying glass, you will see at the tip of our abdomen (which is arched) a wet pink membrane. That's our scent gland. It's called a Nasonov gland.

From day 12 to about day 35, we build cells and shape the honeycomb. This is when our wax glands, which produce royal jelly, have atrophied. Our wax glands are in our abdomen. Here's another time when beekeepers help us. So we have somewhat of a symbiotic relationship. The beekeeper can install prefabricated wax honeycombs so we don't waste our time and energy building them.

During this time, we house bees build wide cells for drones, small cells for worker bees, and elongated cells for queens. The orientation of queen bee cells differs from drones and female workers. While drones and worker bee cells are horizontal, the queen bee cells are vertical. Although the queen chooses the cells she deposits her eggs in, we worker bees determine not only the size of the cells but also the ratio between drones and worker bees. We do this when spring approaches.

I do guard duty from the eighteenth to the twenty-first day, which is my last duty as a house bee. This is when my stingers and my venom sac develop.

My position as a guard is at the entrance to the hive. We guard bees check everyone's scent before we let them in our hive. If we allow bees from another hive to enter, they won't stay long. They sample our wares and go. Of course, sometimes we'll take a bribe (nectar and pollen). Saints we ain't.

Guarding is another dangerous task. Sometimes an invader tries to rob us by sneaking past us. We girls will fight an intruder if it kills us, and sometimes it does. We have to defend our colony. If we don't, the invader will take all our food which, of course, means we are doomed. We become very nasty and very aggressive. Our beekeeper becomes more wary of us.

When we're between twenty-two and forty-two days old, we become field bees. Since we only live about six weeks, our lives are half over. We pack a lot of living in that short time. Now I can fly out of the hive and forage for pollen, nectar, and water which I carry back to the hive.

Although our lives are short in summer, we live longer in winter (about four to eight months). Of course, when spring comes, we're fat. (Too much food yet too little exercise makes us fat—just like you.)

So that's what our jobs are.

Here are some more facts about our duties in a hive.

We have to have cells with eggs. If we don't and we have a beekeeper, the beekeeper brings us a queen. If not, then we worker bees will create cells. This can occur when our queen produces fewer eggs or we don't have a queen. Queen bee egg production usually begins to wane after about a year because her pheromones decrease. This lets us know it's time for a new queen. Without a queen, there would be no colony.

We can lay eggs before we're three weeks old. Because beekeepers inspect us all the time, they can tell if the queen bee is missing, if there are a lot of drones, and if there are two eggs in a cell.

When they see a lot of drones and two eggs in a cell when there should only be one, they know they have laying worker bees. That's a serious problem. They will get rid of laying worker bees *muy pronto*.

CHAPTER 10
COMMUNICATION

We communicate with chemical scents called pheromones secreted by exocrine glands. Pheromones have a pleasant odor and are very important to us. They give our hive a perfume scent. Bee larvae, pupae, the queen, drones, and worker bees have pheromones. Broods and combs have pheromones.

Pheromones are how we recognize gender, stage of development, and feeding needs. Foraging bees use pheromones to guide them. When we release our pheromones, our behaviors change.

We have egg-marking pheromones so we know which eggs are deposited by our queen and which are by laying worker bees. Our pheromones slow down the maturing process in order to keep a balance between drones' and worker bees' activities in our hive.

When the queen's pheromones decrease or her egg laying is reduced, a beekeeper has to act. He'll clip one of her legs so she can't place her eggs in a cell. We worker bees recognize this and will rear a replacement queen. Beekeepers don't care very much for this. It's hard for them to introduce a replacement queen in the cell.

Pheromones are necessary for another reason. Without the queen's pheromones, our reproductive organs go into overdrive. Then we produce nonfertilized eggs, which means only drones will hatch. If this goes on for any length of time, our hive is doomed. So pheromones inhibit us from making drones by preventing development of our ovaries and therefore we can't lay eggs.

MY LIFE AS A HONEY BEE

Pheromones keep our colony together. They let us know when an intruder is present and when our queen is present. It's the pheromones that make us aggressive. Pheromones allow the queen to attract drones. We have alarm pheromones that let us scent-mark our food sources and scent-mark the location and pheromones that tell my sisters when I'm stinging someone and come help me. The queen's pheromones signal when it's time to swarm and to warn queens-in-waiting they have a rival. Pheromones let us know when to get busy comb building, brood rearing, foraging, and storing food.

CHAPTER 11
HOW WE RECOGNIZE EACH OTHER

If you were to peer into my hive, how could you tell a worker bee from a drone or a queen bee? Or a virgin queen?

We female bees are so numerous we can't be missed. We overwhelm the other bees just because there are so many of us. We're smaller than the queen bee, and our bodies are long, but not as long as the queen's. We have three ocelli (eyes) which are a bit larger than the queen's. We are also far more active than either our brother drones or the queen.

It's easy to recognize drone cells. They are wider than the others. Drones' middles are barrel shaped. Another way to identify drones is by their eyes, which are huge and wrap around their heads. They also have three ocelli. We all have ocelli. Ocelli are sensitive to light and help us see in our dimly lit hive. Drones don't have pollen baskets or stingers. They live about three months. There are fewer drones (about 5–10 percent of the population in any hive than worker bees).

The queen produces drones when she chooses not to fertilize an egg. (So drones have no father.) We take care of drones just as we do the queen. The drones' job is to mate with the queen. Their mating takes place in flight about two hundred to three hundred feet off the ground and may be as much as a mile from the hive. Once the mating is complete, the drone dies. When the weather gets cold, we have to shoo the surviving drones out. They consume too much food so they have to go.

How can you recognize the queen? She develops in a cell that is larger than the others. About the sixteenth day (or earlier), she emerges from her cell. The queen is the longest bee and the one most narrow. Like drones, she will not have a pollen basket on her hind legs. They are not foragers so they have no need for pollen baskets. However, she has a stinger. Her stinger is not barbed so she can sting many times. She also has ocelli. Of the three of us, her ocelli are the smallest.

The queen bee is the most important bee in our hive. Without her, there would be no colony. She is totally unable to take care of herself. We workers have to feed and clean her. She never leaves the hive except to mate.

She lays eggs two or three days after mating. Of course, the cells have to be immaculate or she will not deposit her eggs, which are about 0.07 inches long and 0.02 inches wide. They look like rice. If you're looking for her eggs, it's best to search for them on a sunny day with the sun behind you.

A queen doesn't lay eggs in winter. In spring, she'll go from cell to cell laying one egg in a cell, skipping some cells. This is absolutely necessary. It results in a pattern so that we don't all develop at the same time and at the same rate.

She lays her eggs in different-sized cells. So she creates her own demise because she deposits her eggs in the queen bee cells. Our worker bee cells are small, and the queen will deposit a fertilized egg into the cell. Drone cells are larger, and she will not fertilize them.

It isn't known with any certainty how many eggs a queen can lay a minute or a day because it depends on her productivity and how many hours she deposits her eggs. Although a rough estimate of 1,500–3,000 may be realistic. Her only duties are to keep the hive populated and keep us busy so we have a stable hive, which means brood rearing, foraging, comb building, and all the other activities that are so essential for a colony to survive.

There can only be one queen in a hive. Always. If there is more than one, the virgin queens will sting each other until only one survives.

Virgin queens and mated queen bees do, under certain conditions, what is called "piping." Virgin queens "quack" in their cells. Queens "toot" when they're out of their cells.

Piping occurs when there's more than one virgin queen in the hive. It's to let other queens know there's about to be a fight, and it's to let us worker bees know which queen we should support. Piping is also done before swarming.

A virgin queen goes on mating flights and mates with multiple drones. She only has a short time to mate. If there is a delay, such as bad weather, she'll become a drone layer. Again, our colony is doomed.

Virgin queens are smaller than the queen and a little bigger than we worker bees. Their pheromones aren't very strong so we may not recognize them as queens. For that reason, we usually accept them. They are fearless. They run across the comb, climb over us, and fly. They cling to walls or corners. When they emerge from their cells, they look for other virgin queens and attempt to kill them. They'll even kill virgin queens who are inside cells.

CHAPTER 12
OUR DISEASES AND PREDATORS

Despite the fact that we are very clean, we still fall victim to diseases. After all, we're living creatures so we get sick too. But don't worry, our sickness doesn't affect you.

Beekeepers medicate our hive in spring and autumn to prevent diseases by using antibiotics or miticides. The beekeeper waits about four weeks after he's medicated us before harvesting our honey. So the beekeeper is our physician, our caretaker, and anything else! Feral bees must have a lower survival rate because they don't have a beekeeper to take care of them.

We experience colony collapse disease (CCD). No one really knows what causes it. Some possibilities are parasites, pathogens, pesticides, bacterial disease, lack of genetic diversity, and lineage of bees.

For reasons no one has been able to understand, we sometimes abscond—i.e., 100 percent of us leave. When we leave, other insects won't invade our hive. They have no interest in our food. (At other times, we have to guard against them because they'll steal or eat our honey.)

We can be infected with American foulbrood (AFB), which is a bacterial disease. AFB is contagious to bees. It does not affect humans. The disease attacks our larvae and pupae. It can kill our entire colony. So it's the most devastating of our bacterial diseases.

It's easy to tell when we have AFB. Our larvae become tan or dark brown after we are capped. Healthy larvae are white and glossy. The capping looks wet or greasy. There is a terrible odor. Dead brood becomes concave and some look like they have holes. The capped brood pattern isn't compact. The beekeeper has no choice but to destroy our hive.

There is European foulbrood (EFB). The difference between AFB and EFB is that EFB kills larvae before they are capped. The treatment for both is antibiotics.

There is nosema, the most common and widespread of our diseases. It's been recently reclassified as a fungus. Nosema is similar to dysentery in humans. It attacks our stomach lining. The disease weakens us female worker bees more than drones or the queen, who is rarely affected. It can wipe out our entire colony. It happens to us in spring when we come out of our winter period. We are still active in winter, although nowhere near as active as we are in spring and summer. Nosema can reduce the beekeeper's honey production by 40–50 percent.

Symptoms of nosema aren't easy to recognize. Once they become visible, it's probably too late to do anything. We crawl around the front of the hive. There are large numbers of us who die so there is less pollen and nectar gathering. Our feces are seen in and around our hive. A beekeeper will use Fumagilin-B (an antibiotic) in our sugar syrup.

Chalkbrood is a fungal disease. Larvae become chalky white and hard. Sometimes black. Our undertaker bees have to remove them as quickly as possible. I did it when I had undertaker duties.

Damp conditions in spring cause the disease. Although we can take care of it ourselves, the beekeeper helps by cleaning our hive and ordering a new queen.

Stonebrood, another fungal disease, affects our larvae and pupae. The disease doesn't destroy us and is rare. Stonebrood causes the brood to mummify. The beekeeper knows when we have stonebrood because he will see a powdery green fungus covering our brood. We take care of this ourselves by removing dead bees. Again, the beekeeper helps us by removing the bees.

Chilled brood is similar to chalkbrood, but our bodies are soft and translucent. Beekeepers have to be quick in their inspection to avoid losing heat in our hive. If we get cold, we die. Condensation is also a factor that causes chilled brood. We have to have adequate ventilation.

We are affected by viruses that are hard to recognize. Chronic bee paralysis is a virus that is easier to see because we get greasy looking, lose our hair, turn black, and can't fly. We crawl on the grass in front of the hive.

Sacbrood is a viral disease. Like a cold. Our larvae turn yellow and then dark brown. It isn't life threatening. The beekeeper can remove the sac with tweezers. No medication is necessary.

Mite infestations make us more easily susceptible to viruses because they give us wounds that can lead to a viral infection.

Of all our diseases, varroa is the most deadly. Varroa mites are predators. No one likes them. The scent of drones attracts them, and they will invade our brood cells before they are capped. When they do this, they feed on our larvae and pupae. They weaken our hive so we become more susceptible to viruses. They are very small, but the little critters can be seen with the naked eye. They look like ticks. Varroa mites leave brown or reddish spots on our white larvae. We become deformed. They can kill our entire colony in a very short time. When they attach to foraging bees, they can spread to other hives. Those little pests came all the way from Asia.

Beekeepers don't really like to use miticides to get rid of mites because we can build up a resistance to them, and that makes it even more difficult to cure us. They prefer synthetic miticides because they are cheaper and have a high margin of safety. However, whether the beekeeper uses antibiotics, antifungals, or miticides, synthetic or otherwise, we can build up a resistance to diseases.

Beekeepers have to be extremely careful when they treat us so that they don't at the same time contaminate our brood and cause sterility or cause us to abort. Beekeepers have to be extremely careful with temperature control and where they place the miticides. They need to use a treatment that is easy to work with and not disruptive to our colony. Some treatments they use are formic acid and essential oils (such as Apiguard gel). During the treatment time, honey can't be used for consumption. This is bad for the beekeeper.

There are natural treatments that can be used. A powdered sugar (or granulated sugar) shake is used to confirm varroa. In spring and summer, the beekeeper scoops up about half a cup of us and puts us in a jar with a screen in place of a lid. We get shaken very vigorously. Oh, we do not like that! Of course, he won't do this to the queen. Beekeepers, beware when you do this to us. It goes without saying that all the shaking takes place outside the hive. When the beekeeper opens the top, we are so glad to fly back inside. However, once inside, some of that joy is diminished when the house bees start sucking the sugar off us. They love to do that.

One treatment that is effective for viruses and doesn't involve medication is a physical one. The beekeeper shakes us off the frame. Sick bees are too ill to return to the hive. Of course, he has to take care when he shakes us so that healthy bees are not harmed. And of course, the beekeeper won't collect honey for consumption.

We have to guard against tracheal mites. They can't be seen with the naked eye. These parasites attach themselves to our breathing tubes through spiracles, which are holes in the sides of our thoraces and abdomens. Female mites pass through the spiracles into our trachea, lay eggs, and attach themselves to newly emerged bees. These mites easily pass from bee to bee. They can wipe us out. They infest our colony in winter when we aren't active.

Tracheal mites can destroy an entire colony. They are a beekeeper's worst nightmare. Beekeepers know we're sick when they see us stumble about on the floor of the hive. We can't fly. We can't fold our wings, which extend at odd angles. When this happens, we abandon our hive. Completely abscond. Those of us who can, of course.

Tracheal mites can be prevented by using menthol crystals. Of course, we try to remove the crystals because we think they don't belong in our hive. So the beekeeper puts the crystals on aluminum foil. That way, we can't chew holes in them. Menthol crystals can only be used effectively when the temperature is between sixty to eighty degrees Fahrenheit. This is a bit too cold for us. Again, during this time, the honey can't be used for consumption.

The beekeeper can also use sugar and grease patties year round. Sugar and grease patties are the number 1 treatment against tracheal mites. Mites can't reproduce or attach themselves to us.

There are other treatments. But for us, the number 1 treatment is sugar syrup. Of course, some symptoms mimic other symptoms—just like you experience—but we don't have a doctor who can give us all kinds of tests. Our beekeeper has to be very alert and knowledgeable.

Wax moths are a real menace. If we're not aggressive about removing their larvae, they will tunnel their way through our wax comb. We won't be able to get rid of them. Once they take control of our hive, no one can save us. The beekeeper will use PDB (paradichlorobenzene) crystals on the moths and larvae. Sometimes he'll put the frames into a freezer for twenty-four hours. If it's cold enough, the moths will be destroyed.

Then there are black or dark-brown small hive beetles from Africa. We really do hate them. Their larvae eat our wax, pollen, honey, bee bread—i.e., they eat everything. So you see why we don't like them and why we need to get rid of them. We chase them. They hide from us. If we have a vigilant beekeeper, he will build us a two-piece plantar trap with holes and put vegetable oil in the lower trap. The beetles fall through the holes and drown. Don't feel sorry for them. They have no manners and not a shred of decency. They defecate in our honey, which causes the honey to ferment. When that happens, we pack up and go!

Beekeepers use CheckMite+ when the small hive beetle infestation is heavy. They can also use it for varroa mites. Research is being done on what effect CheckMite+ has on us, particularly newly emerged bees and adult drones. It can contaminate the hive. CheckMite+ has to be used with great caution because it contains coumaphos which is used in nerve gas.

Of course, beekeepers check with state agencies so they can determine if the disease is spreading across the country. The state agency also advises what treatment the beekeeper should use.

Luckily for us, beekeepers are constantly researching and experimenting with different substances to keep us healthy. They have an ulterior motive: to ensure we are productive and profitable. We all are very grateful to them for persevering and for everything they do for us.

We bees have lice! They are about 0.59 inches long, reddish brown in color, covered with spine-like hairs, have no wings, sometimes mistaken for varroa mites, and have six legs (varroa mites have eight). They are usually found on the queen's heads. They feed on food in our mouths. They are more of a nuisance than anything else.

Let's not forget ants. They can overrun our colony in no time at all. They must have a phenomenal reproductive rate. They make it necessary for us to leave our colony. One thing a beekeeper does to help us with that problem is to use ground cinnamon at the base or top of the hive because ants don't like it. He can also put dirty motor oil or grease around our hive when it's on a stand with legs. Or he can buy ant powder. Ants don't seem to like pepper very much either.

Bears also like our honey, but they like our larvae even more. They will destroy our hive to get it. They will eat us.

We are not safe from raccoons either. However, they don't eat us. They just rob our hive of honey. Badgers (also known as ratels) also like our honey.

A skunk will eat us! They sneak up to our hive at night and scratch at our entrance. When we come out to see what all the scratching is about, they eat us. Gulp. Gulp. Gulp. It makes us very irritable. They can decimate us. They're too big for us to sting. Think of all that fur and, oh my gosh, the smell! We are very sensitive to odors. Remember, we have 170 odor receptors.

These skunks disturb our sleep and, for foraging bees, that is bad. Why is that? We don't function well when we don't get enough sleep. Being tired affects our accuracy in communicating direction and distance of pollen and nectar. So we're not precise in letting our sisters know where to find food. We're affected by circadian rhythm like you!

If those aren't enough, we can have a mouse in our house in winter. Oh yes. They mark our hive with their urine on cool autumn nights, and then when winter comes, they live with us because our hive is warm and dry. Of course, they make a big mess and usually leave in spring before we come out of our cluster and chase them out or sting them to death.

But sometimes we do dispatch the mouse. Since the mouse is too big for us to carry, we cover it with propolis (brown and sticky bee glue). Propolis has antibacterial and antimicrobial properties. This is why our hive is not contaminated. Since our hive is hot and dry, the mouse becomes mummified. So then we have a mummy mouse in our house!

On top of all these hazards, we have to contend with robbers who invade us from other hives. Robbers are sneaky and are a serious problem. They can destroy us by challenging us guard bees. You will see us lady guard bees at the entrance to our hive valiantly fighting to protect our hive and our honey. We may lose our lives defending our hive. If our guard bees fail to defend the hive, the robbers strip our hive of every morsel of food.

There's a difference between robbing behavior and our normal behavior when we bees return from a foraging foray or from exploring how to find our hive. Or cleaning the entrance to the hive inside and out. So what is the difference?

We have different flying styles. A telltale sign is that robbers fly side to side in front of the entrance and wait for an opportunity to fly past our guard bees. When the robbers leave the hive with honey, they are so loaded down with their trophies (our food) that they can't fly. The little pests have to climb up our hive to take off. Once they're in the air, they dip a little and fly away. They take our food out. We bring our food in.

On the other hand, new foraging bees (as mentioned before) orient themselves to their hive by facing the hive, hovering up, down, back and forth, and flying in circles. Each time they complete a circle, they make a wider circle. They float near the entrance to the hive.

Here's another time when beekeepers prove they're our friends. They make the entrance to the hive large enough for one bee to get in and out or they will stuff grass at the entrance. Of course, they won't cut off our circulation. When the weather is hot and dry, they cover the entrance with a wet bedsheet. We don't have a problem getting in and out. Beekeepers try to prevent robbers by not letting honey in open places and by being careful not to drop sugar syrup anywhere. We keep our beekeeper as busy as a bee!

CHAPTER 13
PROPOLIS

We bees give you propolis, which we collect from tree sap, resin, and balsams. We build hives in tree cavities and seal cracks with it. We also use it to coat branches against ants. We mix it with our saliva and add it to beeswax.

Propolis has antibacterial, antifungal, and antimicrobial properties. That's why it's used to heal wounds and is used as an ointment for cuts, bruises, and abrasions. It can be used for sore throats. Hard to believe, but it can also be used in place of varnish. Isn't it astonishing that propolis and beeswax have so many different uses?

Beekeepers don't like to work with propolis. It's very difficult to remove from the skin. Rubbing alcohol takes it off the skin. But not clothing. To remove it from clothing, beekeepers have to freeze the clothing with the propolis on it. After it's frozen, he whacks it real hard to break it into pieces.

CHAPTER 14
OUR ANATOMY

Since I'm very small, it isn't easy to see my body parts.

So let me describe them to you

My head is oval in shape, flat, and not much bigger than a seed. There's a brain in there. There are glands in my brain that produce royal jelly and pheromones. Like you, my brain regulates my body system and contains sensory organs so I have sight, touch, taste, and smell.

I have two compound eyes, so I see in all directions. And of course, ocelli, which I have already described.

We see images. After all, we have to distinguish different kinds of flowers. We wouldn't be good foragers if we couldn't differentiate between colors and shapes. But mostly we are guided by our highly developed sense of smell. We can thank our pheromones for that.

My skeleton is outside my body. I have a fuzzy body due to hairs. My hairs are sensitive and affected by electrostatic buildup. It's the electrostatic buildup that helps pollen stick to me. It also makes me sensitive to changes in barometric pressure and temperature. We can feel a bit apprehensive when a storm is about to begin.

I have two pairs of wings: one pair in front and one pair in back on my thorax, which is between my head and my abdomen. Can you guess how fast I can beat my wings? Approximately two hundred beats a second! That's why you can hear our buzzing. I fly fifteen miles an hour. We can hook our wings together when we fly and fan them out when we're relaxed.

My legs are highly functional and flexible. I have three pairs of them. Each leg has six segments. Our legs serve many purposes. For example, we have taste receptors on the tips of our legs. (We also have taste receptors on our antennae, pharynx, mouth parts, and feet.) We clean our antennae with our forward legs. We have tibial spurs on our middle legs. We use the spurs to stab wax flakes from glands in our abdomens. The wax is then transferred to our mandibles. Once the wax is in our mandible, we shape and position it on the comb. We use our middle legs to walk and to pack pollen and propolis into our pollen baskets on our hind legs. Our hind legs are covered with hairs as stiff as bristles. It's the hairs that form our pollen baskets. Because our hind legs have combs and pollen presses, we can brush, collect, compress, and carry pollen and propolis to the hive.

We have feet. At the tip of our feet are claws that let us stand on rough surfaces without falling off. We also have soft pads on our feet that allow us to walk and stand on smooth surfaces like glass.

My jaw—i.e., my mandible—is very strong and useful. I use my mandible to pick up debris from the hive, to attack intruders, to manipulate wax in the honeycomb, feed larvae, and distribute food.

I also have an abdomen. That's where my digestive system and reproductive organs are located. My abdomen also is where spiracles (tiny holes) are found on my sides. Spiracles are also on the sides of my thorax. There are tubes in my abdomen that cleanse our system (like your kidneys) and pass the impurities into the intestines, where the poisons are eliminated.

Our abdomen is where our stingers and venom sac are attached. The venom sac looks like a fishhook. It's connected to my barbed stinger. When I sting, my stinger gets lodged in the intruder. I can't pull it loose, so it gets left at the injection site along with parts of my digestive system, my muscles, and my nerves. In other words, my abdominal cavity ruptures, which is what kills me. We're like suicide bombers.

Our hearts are below our abdomens. They have five pairs of openings with one-way valves that circulate our blood.

MY LIFE AS A HONEY BEE

The pharynx is part of our digestive system. It allows us to suck nectar up. It's where some of my taste receptors are.

Our esophagi are part of our digestive system. The esophagus is a thin tube that connects the pharynx and our honey crop (or honey stomach).

The honey crop is used to store nectar until we return to the hive. We don't digest anything in the honey crop. We have a valve that prevents nectar from passing into the true stomach. The crop is expandable.

My true stomach (or ventriculum) is where nectar and pollen are digested. Pollen and nectar combine to form a soupy mass of various shapes. The stomach is coiled around inside my abdomen and is twice the length of my body.

Enzymes and proteins in the honey crop make it possible for us to begin processing nectar while storing it until we get to the hive. In my true stomach, the nectar is transformed into honey.

We have intestines and rectums which are expandable. That's how water is reabsorbed into our bodies. Our hives are clean because we can hold wastes for as long as necessary. That could be months. In spring, we go on a cleansing flight. We won't live in a dirty hive.

We have four exocrine glands in our heads and thoraces that secrete substances through our mouths and aid in digestion.

We have something you don't have: antennae. They are sensory organs and allow us to smell and feel. Two antennae are attached to our foreheads. Antennae let us know our speed and orientation during our foraging flights. We keep them scrupulously clean. If they're dirty, we can't smell right.

We have salivary glands at the front of our thoraces that are connected to our mouths by a duct leading to our heads. The glands produce enzymes that break down sugar and nectar.

The thorax, which is the middle part of my body, is the attachment site for our legs and wings. Our flight muscles are located in the thorax. The thorax is comparable to your chest.

The proboscis can be rolled and unrolled to drink and feed. It's like your tongue. It waves about when we're searching for pollen and nectar.

So you see, each segment has a job to do. All our physical characteristics and activities serve a purpose: to make beeswax and honey. The one you like most is honey.

CHAPTER 15
BEESWAX

How does the beekeeper make beeswax? Our beekeeper slices wax from cappings when he extracts honey. He cleans the wax and melts it down for all kinds of products. Beeswax has no nutritional value, but it's worth more than honey. The beekeeper can get one or two pounds of beeswax for every one hundred pounds of honey.

Beeswax looks like white flakes. It has many products that you use daily. We use the wax to build wax combs and cappings of ripened honey. It's used in such products as lip balm, lip gloss, crayons, furniture and shoe polish, cosmetics, fashion, dentures, crowns, repellents, and soap. You name it. There's probably beeswax in it.

Beeswax is used to make candles that don't drip or smoke. They burn a long time. They also reduce the effects of allergens in the air. Since hives produce different colors of wax, not all candles used will be snow white. Many years ago, the Catholic Church would only use candles made with beeswax. Nowadays, they use paraffin as well as beeswax in their candles. Our beeswax is not cheap.

Of course, you can add different products to our beeswax, such as chamomile, citronella, lemongrass, eucalyptus, herbs, oils, etc.

Another important fact about beeswax is that it's chemical free and has a pleasant odor.

CHAPTER 16
HONEY

Honey is a good source of food not only for bees and animals but also for people. It contains carbohydrates (as high as 82 percent), protein, amino acids, and antioxidants. It also contains B vitamins, minerals (calcium, iron, zinc, potassium, to name a few), and flavonoids. One flavonoid is pinocembrin, which is unique to honey and propolis.

Let me say one more thing about how we make honey.

The process begins with our saliva. Saliva plays an important part in producing honey.

We house bees take the nectar and roll it around our mouths to make the nectar warm which causes some water to evaporate. We eject the nectar through our mouths.

We fan to speed up evaporation which helps to thicken the nectar. This is how nectar becomes honey, which is about 14–18 percent water and 75–85 percent sugar. Eventually the nectar is deposited as honey into combs until the combs are full. Then we seal the honeycomb with a liquid from our abdomen and go on to the next empty comb. The upper part of the comb is where honey is stored. Most pollen is stored in the lower combs where our nursery is located. When the comb is filled with honey and has been capped with beeswax, it's fully ripened. The beekeeper takes the comb away. Needless to say, he is most happy!

During the process of converting nectar into honey, glucose is converted into gluconic acid, fructose, and sucrose, which are simple sugars. There is also a bit of hydrogen peroxide in the mix. When converting nectar into honey, the result is a low pH (between 3.4 to 6.1 with an average of 3.9—it depends on the floral source). Our honey is about as acidic as oranges (3.0 to 4.0) and cherries (3.2 to 4.0). Our acidity is why bacteria, molds, fungi, and microbes don't survive in our honey.

Honey gives energy. Some athletes are advised to eat honey before an event. Honey is 304 kcal, which is equal to 304,000 calories. We bees eat a lot of honey. After all, we are very busy for up to 12 hours or more a day. We need the energy.

CHAPTER 17
MAKING A COLONY: SWARMING

Have you ever wondered how a colony gets started?

One way is by swarming. Swarming is only done when it's necessary. Why do we swarm? There could be many reasons. It's difficult to pinpoint a specific one. Perhaps our queen is lost or is not producing. We may have pests or maybe our colony has gotten too big. Or there could be a ventilation problem.

When it's time for us to swarm, we are programmed to divide in half.

We won't swarm unless the queen bee is mated. When we swarm, the number of capped brood has to be equal to the number of bees swarming. Usually this is in spring or autumn. It's how we manage our growth and survival.

When we swarm, the queen and me and my sisters fly off to create a new colony. The old queen will usually leave before the first virgin queen emerges from her cell. If there is a virgin queen and an old queen, the old queen will probably not be killed since she is near the end of her life. However, if the old queen is still productive, expect a fight.

There's another time when an old queen will be killed. When a new queen is present, we worker bees may kill the old queen. We cluster around her and sting her till she dies. It's called "balling."

Before swarming, we gorge ourselves with honey and cluster around the queen who is in the center of the swarm. We also pipe.

When we swarm, we'll land anywhere and will stay there until our scout bees return with news that they've found a place for a new hive. We move en masse to the new site, build a wax comb, and raise a brood. The new site has to be a protected area and could be anywhere there is a cavity or some sort of hollow. That means it could be your house. If you see us around your house, your best option is to call a beekeeper who will come to smoke us and remove us. The beekeeper will find a place where we can colonize. An exterminator won't. The beekeeper's interest is to keep us alive so we can be productive. The exterminator just wants us gone.

Sometimes our swarm may be small. Other times it can be quite large. But don't forget we are harmless when we don't have a hive to protect. Just leave us be. Sometimes we get riled up. We are a bit territorial.

Beekeepers can tell when we're ready to swarm because we worker bees make swarm cells containing queen egg cells. He'll find the swarm cells in the lower third of the hive. Also, there will be fewer eggs and fewer bees. That tells the beekeeper the bees are ready to swarm. He is not at all happy. It means his honey production will be reduced. It takes a new queen a while to start producing.

The beekeeper tries to prevent swarming by giving us a new queen and cutting out the swarm cells. It's better for him to do that. He'll order a new queen or maybe he'll let the colony raise its own. He knows we won't swarm if we don't have a queen in the making. He'll prevent swarming, give us more room, provide better ventilation, make sure we have water, and keep the hive out of too-bright sun.

If all goes well, he'll have a mated queen who emerges. She will lay eggs. The worker bees will do what they have been ordained to do. He will have a nice honey production and make lots of money. Problem solved!

A beekeeper can capture a swarm and start a new hive. Capturing a wild swarm can be risky. The beekeeper might accidentally include a queen from another hive or an African honey bee. If he has marked the queen, there is not much of a problem.

Capturing a swarm can be easy since we don't have a hive to defend so we are sweet and gentle. He will get a container, sometimes a beehive, sometimes a box—it's just temporary—to hold us. Sometimes all he has to do is remove our colony from a bush or a branch.

If the beekeeper kindly and gently places our swarm into a container, we're fine. But if he is abrupt with us, we can get awfully upset and turn into psycho bees.

A beekeeper can split our hive into two hives if our hive is strong and healthy. It's best to do this in spring to prevent swarming. Two hives are better than one. Of course, he'll have to build a new hive for the division. Sometimes the beekeeper will put a new queen in one of the hives.

MY LIFE AS A HONEY BEE

When the new queen takes up residence in the hive, she may lay only drone eggs. This may be because the queen doesn't successfully mate or she's used up the sperm. The hive is doomed.

To make one hive from two (the beekeeper does this when a hive is weak), the beekeeper combines the two colonies. It's similar to making two hives except he puts the weak colony on top of the stronger colony's hive. Eventually they merge. So then there is more than one queen. Whichever queen is the weaker soon goes.

Sometimes the beekeeper has to smoke us because we can get awfully aggressive when we're disturbed. He will smoke our entrance first, and then he'll smoke us. The smoke hides his scent. It doesn't hurt us. It calms us and turns our alarm pheromones off so we can't communicate "Invader!" "Invader!" Smoke is like your Xanax. Also, when we get smoked, we engorge ourselves with honey in case we have to abandon our hive.

To smoke us the beekeeper starts a fire in a small handheld smoker. He uses anything that is combustible – paper, kindling, some twine, etc. He uses a bellow to blast cool smoke at us in small puffs. It's very much like starting a fire in a fireplace, isn't it?

If we're not smoked enough, here's what happens. We all gather on the top bars of the frame. Hundreds of us. Maybe thousands. We huddle by positioning ourselves in a very close, side-to-side line. We watch the beekeeper. Intently. Our little eyes—all three of them—never leave his face. It's very intimidating. Drum roll please. Or at least a trumpet or two. On your mark! Get set! Go! We must look like little airplanes or helicopters, buzzing and flapping our wings ready to launch an attack.

We have to get ready for winter just like everybody else. We do this in spring and summer and into autumn.

CHAPTER 18
HOW WE WINTER

When autumn approaches, we use propolis to close up cracks and strengthen our comb and hive. A beekeeper protects our hive from the cold by using tar paper and providing ventilation. He provides a windbreak and puts up a mouse guard. He makes sure we have enough food. He feeds us medicated syrup so we not only have enough food but also antibiotics to keep us healthy.

We don't fly very much in cold weather. Some bees, like bumble bees, hibernate. We don't. We huddle together around the queen bee which is in the center of the hive. We keep her warm by shivering. It's also how we keep ourselves warm. Shivering raises our body temperature. Of course, we have to change places so that none of us gets too cold. The colder it is, the closer we get to one another until we are all squished together. Really squished. What helps to keep us warm is honey. We eat honey because it's converted into calories, and heat comes from calories.

CHAPTER 19
OUR FRIEND, THE BEEKEEPER

As to beekeepers. Although beekeepers are our friends, they have this habit of inspecting our hives regularly and frequently. We're not too fond of this activity because they turn our house up, down, and sideways. This pleases us not at all. We see you, Mr. Beekeeper, and if you are not careful, you will get stung. For certain.

Our beekeeper checks us weekly. Why is that? The beekeeper has to know if the hive will survive. He needs to see what is going on inside. Do we have a brood? Are we storing food? Are our cappings and bees healthy? Is the queen present and mated? Is she laying? Are there invaders? What are the worker bees doing? Are there drones and how many? Are there laying worker bees? If so, the laying worker bees will not accept a queen. They will kill her. These are the things he checks. The beekeeper has to know if the hive will survive.

The beekeeper has to be doubly careful in removing laying worker bees. In order for the hive to survive, all laying worker bees have to go—100 percent of them. Just one laying worker bee can obliterate all his efforts. He shakes us to the grass away from our hive. He takes a brush and makes sure none of us hang on the frame or is returning to it. He puts the empty frame into an empty hive that is placed away from the old hive. Eventually, the old frame goes back to the original hive, which already may have bees in it because older foraging bees can find their way back to the hive and newbies can't. Newbies have not oriented themselves to the new hive.

CHAPTER 20
KILLER BEES

Incidentally, you've heard of killer bees, right? They are Africanized honey bees (AHB) and are a subspecies of Apis mellifera scutellata. We belong to the same subspecies. We look exactly alike except through a microscope or a DNA sample.

AHBs came to our part of the world in the 1950s from Brazil by way of South Africa. Some scientists tried to breed them with us in the hopes that the merger would result in us being better adapted to the tropics. Unfortunately, researchers in Brazil lost control of their experiment. Some queens escaped and interbred with us. They reproduced and expanded throughout South America, Mexico, and Southern Texas.

AHBs are more resistant to disease and are better foragers than us. They also swarm more frequently. However, they are difficult to manage, so they aren't as popular in the United States or as useful as we are. Also, they don't produce much wax.

Although AHBs don't tolerate cold climates very well, they can sometimes tolerate up to three and a half months of freezing weather.

They are very quick to defend their hives, and they defend in large groups. They also are long-distance flyers and can outrun you. On top of that, they have a great deal of patience. They will chase an intruder for miles. For heaven's sake, don't head for water when they chase you. They're smart. They know you can't hold your breath forever. They'll just wait until you surface. Try to get inside a building.

Long story short, don't try to capture them. Get a bee supplier or beekeeper.

CHAPTER 21
CODING

When you look into our hive, you'll see the queen bee has a colored dot on her forehead. Why is that? Beekeepers have to mark their queen. When they inspect our hive, they look for an unmarked queen. If she is unmarked, she could be from another hive or she could be an African honey bee. In either case, the beekeeper will remove her.

Another reason for marking the queen is that the mark tells the beekeeper the approximate age of the queen. That's how he can determine how long he can expect her to be productive and when to replace her.

To mark the queen, beekeepers use the International Queen Honey Bee Marking Color Code.

The code is linked to the last digit of the year. It works like this:

1 to 6 is white	Will
2 to 7 is yellow	You
3 to 8 is red	Raise
4 to 9 is green	Good
0 to 5 is blue	Bees

Isn't that cute?

CHAPTER 22
OUR STINGER

By the way, have you ever gotten stung by a honey bee?

Once I put my stinger in a foreign object (like you, for example), my venom continues to pump. When I sting you, don't pinch my stomach. The best way is to take a plastic card or a dull, hard piece of paper (cardboard works very nicely) and scrape the stinger off. Of course, you can also scrape the stinger off with your fingernail. Be sure it's clean. Some people receive more comfort and have less swelling when they take an antihistamine in pill or cream form.

Less than 1 percent of the population is allergic to my venom. In some people, the venom is life threatening. People who are allergic to my venom should carry an EpiPen prescribed by a physician.

Bad as that may be, my venom serves a useful purpose. It's used to treat people with arthritis and other inflammatory medical conditions. A bee sting may help you build up a tolerance for my venom by desensitizing your allergies. Wildflowers from local flowers are especially good for people with pollen allergies.

When bees are used to treat health problems, it's called apitherapy.

I could not end my story without mentioning the most interesting thing that is going on between researchers and us female worker bees.

CHAPTER 23
RESEARCH

I could not end my story without mentioning the most interesting thing that is going on between researchers and us female worker bees.

Believe it or not, researchers have experimented with us to see if they could use us instead of sniffer dogs. I hope you find this interesting.

The Defense Advanced Research Laboratory (DARPA) at Los Alamos National Laboratory in New Mexico created the Stealthy Insect Sensor Project in 1999 to teach us how to sniff for bombs. (Wasps were also used, but honey bees were preferred. Maybe they used wasps because we evolved from them. Wasps are predatory. I really don't know.) Their findings were published on December 7, 2006, in the *Biomedicine News* under the title of "Using Bees to Detect Bombs."

Researchers used the Pavlovian conditioning technique on us. The Pavlovian technique is a stimulus-reward system. They know we have 170 odor receptors and wanted to determine if our odor receptors were strong enough and sensitive enough to detect minute substances used in bombs, like dynamite, C-4, TNT, TATP, etc. So they tested us by providing a stimulus (the chemicals in bombs) and the reward (sugar water). What they discovered was that we learned faster than dogs! It only took two to three hours for us to be trained, and besides that, we could recognize lower doses of the concentrate used in the experiment even when chemical odors were masked by other products such as insect repellent or motor oil. (Didn't I tell you we are a very useful and intelligent insect?) Of course, some of us bees are better at detecting minute particles than others.

The researchers trained us to swarm around scents used in bombs. They strapped us into small tubes. (That took a lot of patience and determination.) Researchers used monitoring equipment because when we pollinate, our proboscis waves about to find nectar and pollen. That motion can be picked up by digital cameras and pollen recognition software. The monitor equipment, being portable, can be used in places like airports, subway stations, theaters, and so on.

The devices worked well in small outdoor areas where an observer could follow our path. In large areas like war zones, we had to be fitted with radio transmitters.

There's always a positive and a negative side to everything. The negative side is that when researchers strapped us into their little tubes, we only lived about two or three days. We usually live about six weeks.

The government is not the only organization interested in our odor-detecting capability.

Sometime around 2002 or 2003, researchers at the University of Montana experimented with bee colonies using free-flying bees that circle an area. They used audio, video, and laser systems to analyze flight patterns and were able to produce a density map that indicated the location of chemicals associated with bombs. However, free-flying bees don't work well in airports.

MY LIFE AS A HONEY BEE

During the Yugoslav Wars (1991-2001) thousands of mines were placed in Croatia. Since 1991 an estimated 2500 people have died or were maimed. Probably not all the mines have been discovered.

Croatian scientists experimented with us to sniff out land mines. They released swarms of us and used a heat-sensory camera to track our movements hidden below soil. The good old Pavlovian procedure was used. A little sugar water mixed with small amounts of TNT is all we need to sniff out the TNT in mines. It takes such a minimum amount of time for us to learn. Much less time than it takes to train a dog or a rat. Oh, yes, they tried training dogs and rats because they are supposed to be smart. Well, it seems we're smarter!

Croatian scientists believe that honey bees will discover mines that have been missed and unlike dogs and rats we will not set off the mines because we weigh about 1/10 of 1 gram or 90 mg which is about 1/300 of an ounce. Practically nothing

Scientific researchers at the University of Cologne trained honey bees to tell the difference between heroin and cocaine. They give us the odor of the drug with some sugar water. Once again, we learn in no time at all how to distinguish the odors.

If you're asking yourself can bees become addicted to drugs, the answer is YES!. We can also become addicted to pesticides like you become addicted to nicotine in cigarettes.

I have even heard that researchers are experimenting with us to determine if we can detect certain kinds of cancer!

There are many other organizations researching our sniffing ability and determining if we are scientifically reliable. I am confident that with more research, a way will be found that will benefit all of us.

We don't mind helping you when you use us to defend yourselves, but please, we are not expendable! So, first find a way to let us live our lives and then find a way to let us help you. We honey bees have been around a long time. We want to be here forever. Take care of us, and we will take care of you.

CHAPTER 24
IN CONCLUSION

You will see our name spelled as one word or as two words. Like honeybee or honey bee. Which is correct?

There is the dictionary spelling which newspapers and other nonscientific publications use. And then there is the spelling used by the Entomological Society of America (ESA). The ESA states if an insect is a true insect—i.e., if it belongs to a specific order—it should be spelled as two words. The order we belong to is Hymenoptera.

A honey bee is really a bee as scientists classify it. So are bumble bees. So they are spelled as two words. Dragonflies, for example, are not true flies. They're not true dragons either. So they are spelled as one word. A house fly is really a fly according to entomologists. Hence, it's spelled as two words. A bumble bee is a true bee, so it's spelled as two words. A silverfish is not really a fish. Neither is a cuttlefish really a fish. So they're both one word. As a matter of fact, a cuttlefish is actually a mollusk. It's closely related to slugs and snails that you find in your garden. Science has rules for everything, doesn't it?

I would like to leave you with a question. If you were a honey bee, would you want to be a worker bee? A queen? A drone? Or would you rather be a beekeeper? Or a honey bee researcher?

BIBLIOGRAPHY

Blackiston, Howland. Housekeeping for Dummies. 2nd ed. New Jersey: Wiley Publishing Inc., 2009. Borror, Donald J., and Richard E. White. A Field Guide to Insects: America North of Mexico. Boston: Houghton Mifflin Company, 1970.

Chinery, Michael. How Bees Make Honey. New York: Benchmark Books, Michael Cavendish Corporation, 1997.

Dott, Robert H., Jr., and Roger Batten. Evolution of the Earth. New York: McGraw-Hill, 1981.

Ellis, Katherine. "The Basics of Bees," research paper, Houston Museum of Natural Science, Houston, TX, _____.

Ellis, Katherine. "The Anatomy of a Worker Bee and Other Bee—related Facts," research paper, Houston Museum of Natural Science, Houston, TX, _____.

Land, Benjamin B., and Thomas D. Seeley "The Grooming Invitation Dance of the Honeybee," research paper, Department of Neurobiology and Behavior, Cornell University, Ithaca, NY, 2004. Waldbauer, Gilbert. Fireflies, Honey, and Silk. Berkeley, CA: University of California Press, 2009. NY.

Web Sources:

animalcorner.org/animals/bumble-bee, accessed 7-17-2020.

answers.yahoo.com/question/index?qid, accessed 7/17/2020.

bbc.com/uk,newsbeat/article33195468/honey-bees-trained-to-detect-illegal-drugs, accessed 7/16/2020.

beehivehero.com/what-do-bumble-bees-eat, accessed 7/17/2020.

beekeepercenter.com/do-bumble-bees-make-honey, accessed 7/17/2020.

extreme.tech.com/extreme 156259-honeybee-trained-to-sniff-out-land-mines-might-replace-sniffer-dogs-in-airports, accessed 7/17/20.

Healthline.com/nutrition/raw-honeycomb, accessed 7/12/2020.

honeybeesuite.com/why-do-brood-combs-turn-black, accessed 7/17/2020.

livescience.com/38242-why-honeybees-honeycombs-are-perfect.html, accessed 7/12/2020.

morningchores.com/what-do-wasps-eat, accessed 7/17/2020.

sciencefriday.com/educational-resources/why-do-bees-build-hexagonal-honeycomb-cells, accessed 7/12/2020.

sciencing.com/do-wasps-make-nests-547075.1html, accessed 7/17/2020.

smithsonianmag.com/innovation/can-bees...., accessed 7/15/2020.

http://en.wikipedia.org/wiki/Bees, accessed 8/20/2011.

http://en.wikipedia.org/wiki/Greater_honeyguide, accessed 3/29/15.

http://en.wikipedia.org/wiki/Honey_bee, accessed 12/29/2013.

http://en.wikipedia.org/wiki/honeycomb, accessed 7/12/2020.

http://en.wikipedia.org/wiki/Nosema_apis, accessed 1/3/2015.

http://en.wikipedia.org/wiki/Propolis, accessed 7/26/2020.

http://en.wikipedia.org/wiki/Queen-bee, accessed 7/19/2014.

http://en.wikipedia.org/wiki/Tremble_dance, accessed 5/4/2014.

http://missapismellifera/com/tag/sickle-dance, accessed 7/2/2014.

http://science.howstuffworks.com/bomb-sniffing-Bees-html, accessed 4/29/2015.

http://scienceline.org/2007/04/ask-westlv, accessed 4/7/15.

http://scientificbeekeeping.com/miticides_2011, accessed 1/3/2015.

http://technologyreview.com/news/406961, accessed, 12/29/2015.

http://wiki.answers.com/Q/What_vitamins_are_in_honey..., accessed 5/11/2014.

http://www.backyardbeekeeping101.com/ants-in-beehive, accessed 7/20/2020.

http://www.bee-pollen-health.com/how-do-bees-make-honey, accessed 12/21/2013.

http://www.beehivetutorial.com/queens-worker-and-drone-brood, accessed 7/20/2020.

http://www.beekeepinglikeagirl.com/how-to-protect-your-bees, accessed 7/20/2020.

http://www.benefits-of-honey-com/how-do-bees-make-honey.html, accessed 12/21/2013.

http://www.bumblebeeconservation.org/bee-faqs/finding, accessed 7/17/2020.

http://www.chm.bris.ac.uk/webprojects2001/loveridge.index-html, accessed 7/19/2014.

http://www.dave-cushman.net/bee/cellsize.html, accessed 5/10/15.

http://www.dave-cushman.net/bee/weathersense.html, accessed 7/5/2014.

http://www.ehow.com/how-does_5611646_do_honeybees_pollin..., accessed 5/11/2014.

http://www.extension.org/pages26930/dance-language-of-the-honey-bee, accessed 7/2/2014.

http://www.getbuzzingaboutbees.com/honey-bee..., accessed 6/24/2015.

http://www.gpnc.org/honeybee.html, accessed 8/20/2011.

http://www.honey.com/nhb/about-honey/honey-and-bees, accessed 8/13/2011.

http://www.honeybeesuite.com/bumble-bees-hibernate, accessed 7/17/2020.

http://www.honey-well.com/composit.html, accessed 7/19/2014.

http://www.honeybeesuite.com/how-acid-is-honey, accessed 6/15/2015.

http://www.honeybeesuite.com/tag/scopa/, accessed 5/4/2014.

http://www.honeybeesuite.com/water-collection, accessed 12/18/2014.

http://www.ibra.org.uk/article/miticides..., accessed 2/17/05.

http://www.insectidentification.org/external-anatomy-of-honeybees, accessed 5/15/15.

http://www.livescience.com/4605-bees-trained-bomb-sniffers.html, accessed 6/24/15.

http://www.ncbi.nlm.nih.gov/pmc/articles/PMC2269714, accessed 5/27/2015.

http://www.researchgate.net/publication/227517043 The Grooming Invitation Dance of Honey Bees..., accessed 5/11/2014.

http://www.quora.com/do-wasps-make-honey-or-any-similar, accesssed 7/19/2020.

http://www.sciencing.com/do-wasps-make-nests-5470751.html, accessed 7/19/2020.

http://www.scientificamerican.com/article/face-recognition-hone..., accessed 5/11/2014.

http://www.scienceline.org/2011/03/sleepy-honeybees-dancesloppily, accessed 5/18/2014.

http://www.smithsonian.com/science-nature/the-science-behindhoney-eternal-shelf-life, accessed 5/15/15.

http://www.honeybeesuite.com/why-do-brood-combs-turn-black, accessed 7/17/2020.

http://www.strategypage.com/militaryforums..., accessed 5/30/2015.

http://www.telegraph.co/uk/science/2018/08/28/bees, accessed 7/19/2020.

http://www.theguardian.com/science/2008/dec/23/cocaine, accessed 7/19/2020.

http://www.yaledailynews.com/blog/2012/11/06/..., accessed 1/10/15.

Video

http://www.youtube-nocookie.com/embed/xHkq/edcbk4?rel=o, accessed 6/8/2014.

http://www.cals.ncsu.edu/entomology/apiculture/Dance-Language/ Tutorial.swf..., accessed 5/18/2014.

CPSIA information can be obtained
at www.ICGtesting.com
Printed in the USA
LVHW070141211020
669312LV00040B/2042